I AM UNIQUE

Poems to Inspire
Self-Belief

SUE WILLIAMS

First published in 2017

ISBN-13:978-1973791676

ISBN-10:1973791676

PRAISE FOR *I AM UNIQUE*

The perfect anthology of poems; Sue's book couldn't have arrived at a better time as the feminine energy on our planet rises and more and more women are finding their unique voice. Let these beautifully crafted words sink deep within your soul. Whether you read from cover to cover or dip in and out, this collection will gently nudge you to look creatively at the essence of your own self-expression and most heartfelt dreams.

Allison Marlowe - founder of
Global Winning Women

Sue has woven a rich tapestry of poems, and each one inspires from the heart. What struck me most about this poetry anthology is the many different expressions of self-belief that come through the work. Sue takes you on a journey from really taking stock of life and beginning an emergence of self-belief, all the way through to awakening and embracing your feminine power. If you are on a journey of deeply developing your own self-belief, this unique set of poems will be a perfect accompaniment to each stage of your journey.

Sasha Allenby - author of
Write an Evolutionary Self-Help Book

I Am Unique is a wonderful series of poems which takes you on a journey of transformation you will never forget. It is the confidence boost you need to start believing in your own beautiful uniqueness. I loved it!

Hannah Davis - award-winning author of
Voices of Angels

Be aware there are people who walk the earth carrying a magical butterfly net ever watchful for all those enchanting words winging through the air. Sue Williams is one of these extraordinary individuals with the skill and talent to mindfully catch these words and then thoughtfully release them on the page. Her poetry is the place where they light, then take wing again to carry you along on a wondrous flight of self-discovery into her unique world and your own.

Gwen Anne Duffy – author of
HeartString Theory

Sue is a living, breathing example of the joyful creativity available to any one of us if only we dare to express ourselves. She encourages her readers to explore and express their own worlds, finding beauty in everyday situations, and shows that it's never too late to discover the artist within you.

Alison Jones – author of
This Book Means Business

I Am Unique is a book full of wonderful poems that touches your soul. As you travel alongside with Sue, you're encouraged and empowered to take the next step on your journey, whatever that may be. These inspiring verses will become a starting point for your own self-belief, self-reflection, and will motivate you to keep on writing.

Kylie Holmes – mum and author of
There's No Such Thing as Monsters

If you ever find yourself thinking: "There's got to be more to life than this", Sue's poems are for you! They will provide a beacon of light for women who want to take charge of their lives. They highlight Sue's own journey with self-belief, and how she reconnected to her own creative inspiration through her poetry.

Although an intensely personal journey, there are elements that will empower women everywhere.

Gillian Holland - medium and author of
Flowers Light Up Your Life – Connecting to
Spring with Flowers

As ever, Sue has produced some thoughtful pieces. I remember once, from a throwaway comment on Facebook, she wrote a brilliant poem for me. It is wonderful to see this book published. Grab a cuppa and a slice of something nice and lose yourself.

Jacqui Malpass – author of
The Conscious Woman's Guide to Leaving her
Husband and Getting a Life

Sue takes us on her creative progression from tentative early verses to finding her true authentic, poetic voice. I'm sure she will inspire others to follow suit.

Christine Ingall – author of
Solo Success! You CAN do things on your own

CONTENTS

DEDICATIONS   10

INTRODUCTION

My Journey with Poetry   11

TAKING STOCK

I Reached the Age of Fifty Plus   18

Believe!   20

The Journey   23

BEGINNINGS

All About the Boy   26

Deadened Down There   28

Silent Families   29

Artless Youth   30

Listen to Me, Mummy   31

Lost in the Teapot   33

I AM UNIQUE

I Am Unique   36

The Artist Unmasks   39

Life's Uniform   41

Cosmic Dancer   42

Unleashed   43

The Art of Doing Nothing   44

Who Am I?   46

LOVE

Urban Kiss   48

The Wonder of Love   49

The Womb   50

My Beautiful, Bonny Baby   52

Love   53

Always There   54

LETTING GO

Labels   56

Dig Deep   58

Release, Release   60

The Mask Removed   61

Movement   63

Father's Day   64

An Airlock in Time   66

Slay the Lineage   68

Endings   70

Weighed Down   72

Shine for Me   74

The Tudor Gallery   75

The Divine Tapestry of Life   77

EMERGENCE

Nothing to Say   80

Spring Free   82

Melt Polar Ice Caps   83

A Blank Page   85

Words Matter   86

Flowing Free   88

Locked Away   89

The Grand Canyon   90

AWAKENING

Awaken   94

Riding the Carousel   96

Creating Space   98

Room to write   99

Opportunities   101

Coin   102

Beautiful Beams of Humanity   103

CREATIVE SELF-EXPRESSION

Banish Your Blues 106

Words, words, words 108

Poetic Licence 110

Facebook Fantasies 112

A Swirl of Creativity 115

Gratitude 118

Encapsulated in the Clouds 120

FEMININE POWER

Reclaiming Me 122

The Open Road 124

A Feminine Fanfare 126

We Gather 127

Your Signature Success Story 128

Wow-full Women, Ignite Your Light! 130

I See You 132

Celebration 135

Celebrating You 136

ABOUT THE AUTHOR

ABOUT THE AUTHOR 140

About the Front Cover – The Mask 142

Sue Williams' Books 143

DEDICATIONS

Creating any book is a team effort. There are many people who I wish to thank for their help and support with this one.

First and foremost, to Hannah Davis, for her insight, support and encouragement, and that of the members of her Soul Writers' Café Advanced Mentoring and Accountability Group. Particular appreciation to Gwen Chater, for being my biggest fan and advocate!

Special thanks to my good friend Christine Ingall for reading and reviewing poems with me, and for her thought-provoking suggestions.

To Juliette Jeanclaude, visual artist, for the clown face painting.

Grateful appreciation to Nirmala Patel for copy editing, to Maureen Brindle and Jackie Thompson for their help with formatting, and all those who read and commented on the draft book for their valued help and reassurance. You know who you are!

And finally, to you the readers. I wish you joy on your unique journeys to self-belief and creative self-expression!

❖

MY JOURNEY WITH POETRY

"Let us be lovely and let us be kind. Let us be silly and free. It won't make us famous, it won't make us rich. But dammit how happy we'll be!" - Edward Monckton

Morning Pages

Aged 52, an enthusiastic coach encouraged me to write "morning pages", a technique for free writing pioneered by Julia Cameron in her iconic book, *The Artist's Way*. Reluctantly, I agreed to trial this system. Imagine my surprise, when after approximately 10 days of dutifully writing three pages of free-flowing writing each morning, automatically, my words began to rhyme!

Without warning, I experienced a playful sensation, as sentences flowed, although they were quite meaningless to begin with. And then, suddenly, one morning, as I sat scribbling in my pyjamas, a knight in shining armour, sword flashing, metal crashing, strode onto the scene out of nowhere.

He subsequently muscled his way through three or four stream-of-consciousness verses. It was as if I had been transported back in time, reliving some past life derring-do! And you will see him here too, as he pops up in "Slay the Lineage". I believe he came along to banish my doubts and constriction, and to clear a space to allow me the freedom to play with words and to find my voice.

Beginnings

What you don't yet know is that I had always had difficulty in expressing my innermost feelings. At around the ages of eight to twelve, I kept a daily diary. Back then it was beyond me to express any emotion. There were pages and pages adorned with short, factual sentences about what I had done at school, or watched on the television. During my subsequent career, writing tended to be of the everyday variety, or producing contracts and written reports. No need for emotional expression there!

Although I had "studied" poetry briefly at school, it was only at the bare minimum level required. Generally speaking, it didn't resonate with me. In fact, it often seemed like gobbledy-gook on the page. So, between the day we breathed a sigh of relief and handed in our tatty school textbooks, to when I took early retirement from work, I gave it little further thought. Yet one day, in my early fifties, I began writing again.

Poetry, in reality they are verses although I choose to call them poems, and hope you will be happy to allow me, soon became more than just scribbles in my notebook. It became a means for recording certain events in my life.

I was filled with wonder as I discovered how writing in rhyme helped me to express my hidden emotions, and to release pent-up feelings. The dawn of Father's Day one year reminded me of my dad, and I wrote about how he had slipped away from life as unobtrusively as he had lived. Like him, I was born into a "Silent Family" with a tradition of being quiet and dutiful…

Poems became the backdrop to my life during this time and it has been hugely liberating to express myself in this way.

The Power of a Poem

My initial stream-of-consciousness rhymes were very much of a private nature. I hadn't dared show them to more than a few people, and so a defining moment for me came when I agreed to compile a book of true life stories and poems for an event aimed at women. The event was called *"Believe in Your Dreams, Your Legacy, Your Power."*

In preparing for this venture, one morning, a spark set alight inside of me, words flowed onto the page, miraculously forming a poem "Believe!" One of the lines in the Believe! poem reads: *"You are a beacon shining bright, birthed to emerge, grow, and shine your inner light."*

And so, I wrote the Believe! poem as a clarion call both to myself and to other women who may have experienced a dutiful, compliant upbringing – to have confidence in ourselves, our dreams and aspirations. We all have that beacon inside of us, yearning to be set free. A beacon of hope that will light up the path for ourselves and others, and make meaning out of the pressures of everyday reality.

True North

Often, it can be difficult to find true north, the thing that keeps us on track and encapsulates our hopes, dreams and desires. The Believe! poem became this for me. It provided my own personal moment to *"Stand up, stand up! Be bold, be strong"* when I read the poem aloud on stage at an event for 200 women. It also spurred me on to commit to, and collate, my first book of true stories: *Believe You Can Succeed.* This is a collection of inspirational stories, hints and tips, by myself and other authors, aimed at inspiring women to have the belief to achieve their desires. A second volume, *Believe You Can* has since followed.

I am Unique – Poems to Inspire Self-Belief by Sue Williams

Fast forward to now, and this particular collection of poems. I've included my signature poem, "Believe!", as it is still at the heart of everything I do and teach. Some of the other poems included in this selection capture aspects that women don't always consider during our day-to-day lives, such as the need to take time out to relax and reflect in "The Art of Doing Nothing", to recognise and capitalise on our "Opportunities", to "Celebrate" our successes and express "Gratitude".

Believe It's Your Time

I have written this book of poems for other women, who like me, *"have sometimes been, squashed, ignored, or diligently working; self-effacing, behind a screen of uniformity"*. You most likely carry the weight of past generations on your shoulders, and have now reached a point in your life where you find yourself thinking "There must be more to life than this?" You feel ready to do more for you. You believe it is *your* time.

Perhaps you have had a family, the kids have left home, and you want to take time out to explore your own creativity and purpose? Or, it could be that you are ready to take a step back from a busy job, constant to-do lists and to take time to explore your own creativity, uniqueness and sense of self-expression? Poetry can also be a great way to vent your feelings and emotions, and heal some of the past hurts and pain that you may have carried with you over the years.

Some of the poems in the book, such as "All About the Boy", "Slay the Lineage" and "An Airlock in Time" suggest this pain may have been passed down through the family line... I know my own mother struggled with not having been born a boy, and having to give up work as soon as she became pregnant with my elder brother, her first child. You may wish to review what influences have impacted on your life thus far.

Through this collection of poems, I want to inspire other women to break free from restraint, to have the belief to explore their own dreams and desires. I uncovered my latent creativity, my voice and sense of self-expression in my fifties. Who knows what is possible for you? See what thoughts and feelings are sparked by reading through this book. It may be that poems like "Who Am I?", "Your Signature Success Story", and "Celebrating You" spark you to think about your own strengths, and to claim your own feminine power. Or, you may just decide to "Banish Your Blues" by grabbing a handy paintbrush, and allowing it to "run rife!".

Enjoy the Ride

On a purely personal level, I have found the experience of writing poems and verses has helped me to work through past insecurity and stuffed down emotions. The knight boldly cleared a space for me to reclaim me, and gave me permission to write freely. And so, a number of poems in this collection also focus on the struggle to feel a sense of self-worth, identity, and self-belief; to shake off "Labels", the expectations of society and to claim our own power and unique voice. This can be a journey that takes us deep inside. So often, a lack of inner self-belief can stifle our outward creative self-expression.

I revisit memories and milestones on my own journey of self-discovery from growing up as a sensitive child, experiencing an "Artless Youth", to the playful exploration of clown face painting in my fifties, when the mask I habitually wore was finally removed – "The Artist Unmasks". Taking time out in nature, and observing your dreams "Encapsulated in the Clouds" is also wonderful for providing a sense of renewal, and creative inspiration.

Creativity and Connection

We are also inextricably linked to other people and our surroundings. A number of verses are inspired by events in other people's lives, such as "My Beautiful, Bonny Baby", written for the coach who set me off on the journey of writing morning pages. Two poems about the womb, "Deadened Down There" and "The Womb" were written after a conversation with a participant on a writing retreat I attended, who talked about her work with women.

Others are a response to artworks, such as "Urban Kiss" inspired by a picture posted on Facebook by Lisa Cherry, one of the authors in *Believe You Can*, and "The Tudor Gallery" written after a trip to the National Portrait Gallery in London. Inspiration to explore our creativity is around us all of the time – we just need to give ourselves permission to express ourselves and, above all, to play!

I wish the interplay of creative expression to continue by encouraging others to respond to the thoughts, feelings and emotions prompted by reading these verses. To reflect on how creativity features in your own lives, and to pick up your pen and see what emerges.

Poetry offers the opportunity to explore what is really going on under the surface, to think outside of the lines. It can also be a great way to express ourselves and to connect to others through our creativity. *"And as we choose to change how we ourselves perceive, in our own dreams, our legacy, our power, we truly believe!"*

This is an ongoing journey and I invite you to join me, to travel alongside me, to jump on board, and enjoy the ride! My hope is that you will use this book as a starting point for your own self-belief, reflection and writing.

TAKING STOCK

It's a crime to leave talent, dusty on rickety, hidden shelves...

I REACHED THE AGE OF FIFTY PLUS

I reached the age of fifty plus,

Still feeling an awkward wuss.

Carried careless playground scorn;

Worked many years,

Playing out my fears

In a job that made me yawn!

I crossed a chasm,

Felt like a spasm,

That propelled me towards life.

Yet despite some play,

Creativity, along the way;

The past cut into me like a knife.

So how to break loose

From this papoose;

So tightly clawing at freedom?

Untie the strings that bind me in,

And release my inner wisdom?

I'll write a book,

With a powerful hook;

Full of wonderful wit and words.

So, if advice is took

By those who look,

They'll rise above the starving herds

Of cattle, huddled close for comfort.

Strip back the fear, the shiny veneer,

That keeps them warm and safe;

Unleash the passion buried within

That at their hearts does chafe.

BELIEVE!

Stand up, stand up! Be bold, be strong.

Your talent, on a world stage, truly does belong.

You are a beacon, shining bright,

Birthed to emerge, grow, and shine your inner light!

It's a crime to leave talent, dusty on rickety, hidden shelves,

Set out your stall; allow true expression of your amazing inner selves.

Surely, you will experience some discomfort as you stretch,

Far better than staying a self-defeating, self-pitying little wretch?

Rather, as you experience movement, create life-changing shifts,

You will, newly emboldened, dare to share your gifts!

Life is truly meant for us to live; by our own expression, give

To those, like us, who have sometimes been

Squashed, ignored, or diligently working; self-effacing,

Behind a screen of uniformity; water poured on burning fire,

Quashed down, made damp squib of all passion and desire.

And, as others bask in your new golden glow,

It helps for them, also to know, that they have their own miracles

To perform, whether on a stage, or as more often is the norm,

In their own families and communities, through their daily life and deeds.

Do great work; sow and nurture the seeds of positivity, purposefulness and joy, with which we all entered this world to buoy

Up ourselves and others, to manifest the birth-right of our mothers,

As we mix with friends, many others, who enter into life's stratosphere.

They all add dark and shade, maybe cause us to shed a tear,

Perhaps of joy or sometimes pain,

So, ultimately, of our own truth, understanding we gain.

Right here and now, we need to show,

Through heartfelt determination, strength of courage,

We all have the power to foster our own abilities, to grow;

Achieve our birth-right to succeed; root out the dreaded weed

That with stranglehold choked down our well-intentioned schemes,

Left us struggling with dashed hopes; broken, once beautiful dreams.

Meaning-full, join us to create, an interwoven, brilliant picture

With which all can relate! As one voice, stand up and state:

"We are here to live mindfully in this life,

We choose creativity, positive intent over unrewarding strife

And as we choose to change how we ourselves perceive,

In our own dreams, our legacy, our power, we truly believe!"

THE JOURNEY

And now that I know, dare I let it all go?

Tear up that script, that screed, prevention to succeed?

Let it drift downstream, get lost in the surf,

Turf out old dreams, sometimes screams, from long ago;

The nightmares they became.

Allow myself to ease into my flow. Really let go?

The twists, the turns that led me here, suddenly became a
map,

of roads, no longer to be travelled. Now, so clear; unravelled.

What if I take one step, make one choice, state in my OWN
voice,

"I choose a new path". Newly equipped,

Let any twists and turns along the way,

Lead only to a brighter day.

BEGINNINGS

Root out the dreaded weed that with stranglehold,
choked down our well-intentioned schemes...

ALL ABOUT THE BOY

Dumbed down, deadened down,

Sit in silence, feel a clown.

Cry less, be more,

Open wound, weeping sore,

Barbie girl that all adore.

Silent, plastic, nothing more.

Made of elastic, expand and grow,

Let them know you can knit and sew,

Sing, cook, play piano; looks always in place,

Synthetic smile plastered on your face.

Lace hankies, chair covers,

In bed at night, static lovers.

True self, reality smothers.

No mind of your own,

A worthless clone,

A procreator, incubator,

He's off to the pub, "See you later".

Riddled with guilt and self-doubt,

Dutiful role, flawlessly plays out,

Deeply inbred, you cannot flout;

Silenced; urge to scream and shout.

Forever condemned to suppress your joy;

History proclaimed "It's all about the boy".

DEADENED DOWN THERE

I feel deadened, down there,

A distended desert of dreams; unrealised.

Dried out, destitute, a desolation

Of dormant desire.

Cowed by a clinging clamour of stalactites,

Grim reality hangs suspended,

Banished to a barren bat cave,

Where shadowy, silent, sentinels

Stifle the sweet, suffused, sanctity of motherhood.

SILENT FAMILIES

Will you listen to me?

Why daren't I speak?

What is the problem?

What answers do I seek?

I want you to listen to me,

I need to be heard,

Yet I sit in stony silence,

It seems so absurd.

We are a family,

Why don't we gel?

Magnitudes of silence

Resound our inner hell.

No-one expresses

What they truly think;

Sadness, repression:

Can't cause a stink.

I yearn for us to be happy,

To connect and relate,

Yet circumstance has bidden,

It is already too late.

❖

ARTLESS YOUTH

Sat in class; silent, a mouse.

In art, always draw a plain little house.

Doors and windows, cut out of card,

Seeing within, or without; equally hard.

No depth, no meaning, contained in my soul,

Sensitive, scared, protection my goal.

No colour, no curtains, a drab little door,

How to illuminate this sad, sorry bore?

Retreat, travel inwards, taunts try to ignore,

"Leave me alone, can't take any more".

Clumsy, feel judged, unable to break free,

Expectation drowned in a sea of mediocrity

LISTEN TO ME, MUMMY

Listen to me, mummy!

Please, I want you to hear.

You are a beautiful swan,

Not an ugly duckling, weighed

Down with dread and fear.

Listen to me, mummy!

I see you struggle; three kids

Forever under your feet.

Husband working, dawn till dusk,

Life feels so incomplete.

A battle, a fight, sometimes a war,

Family life, slowly, you came to abhor.

Trapped in a cage, energy replete,

Listen to me mummy; sensitive child by your seat.

I feel for you, I know you, though achingly young;

Nerves jangle, brothers fight. Energy rung out,

Like a dishcloth, twisted by the sink. Listen to me,

Mummy. Reach for the kettle, make a reviving drink.

Listen to me mummy! Please listen.

When you criticise me, you criticise yourself.

Conditioning creates barriers, fall into place through stealth,

Not energy of gratitude, true inner wealth.

Listen to me, mummy! Please hear what I say.

We all have answers, locked deep inside.

Listen to me, mummy, I can help you, if you confide.

Listen to me mummy. We all need time to play.

LOST IN THE TEAPOT

I have hidden, small and scared,

All my life, afraid to be heard.

A sugar-coated, protective shell,

Of sweet, fluorescent pink,

Wrapped around a glaring hole,

Filled with black, swirling, murky ink.

Bereft, true nature long since lost;

Cower in damp, dark gloomy hollow.

Fear, retribution, despair and sin,

Soaked in sadness; world-weary sorrow.

Apart from inward, no place to hide,

"It must be me, I'm in the wrong,

Where do I fit in, how do I belong?"

Dumbed-down diamond, buried deep,

Stealthily, through the spout I sneak a peek.

I AM UNIQUE

Set out your stall; allow true expression of your amazing inner selves...

I AM UNIQUE

I am unique,

Only one me,

Expressing myself,

Creatively.

I am a joker,

I am a clown,

Yet, lift up my mask,

I wear a frown.

A frown of worry,

A frown of fear,

Strain of concealing

Many an unshed tear.

I am strong,

I carry on,

Yet, in reality,

I feel so wrong.

I am unique,

Only one me,

Yet I bow down

To conformity.

The need to be perfect,

The need to fit in,

Afraid of mistakes,

Meaning others will win.

I suppress my feelings,

Experience inner guilt and shame,

When I can't cope,

Always myself that I blame.

Surely there's an answer,

A more feminine way,

Energy free flowing,

Hearing what my heart has to say?

I am unique.

Only one me.

Opening myself

Up, expressively.

THE ARTIST UNMASKS

Does she see through me?

This artist; brush strokes, bold

And deft; eyes flicking back and forth,

Between easel, and face unseen.

Jaw clenched; a defence,

Against? What, exposure?

Does she see inside my soul?

My eyes turn cold, impenetrable

As ice. A mechanistic device.

My face, truly a picture of daubs and smears;

Multi-coloured mask. Appeared, once dance

Had loosened; banished fear! Led me to smooth,

Daub and brush, an extra layer, multi-faceted blush.

This mask I wear, my second skin.

Yet, will I let her in? Unnerved by thought,

Teeth clenched, chin so taut;

Unbidden bursts forth a grin!

Chink in tight-lipped armour.

Dentist's chair springs to mind,

A far more tortuous fate to find!

She smiles too, this artist, distracted.

The magic of soul connection – or my grin refracted?

Refocussed, eyes dart once more.

I, resigned, wait to see…

How insightfully has she captured me?

LIFE'S UNIFORM

Where lies the answer

Behind life's uniform?

Only inside of you,

You are not the norm.

COSMIC DANCER

Leap with joy, pirouette with grace; pure, liquid emotion

Illuminates sweep of soft night sky. Gregarious grand jeté,

Propelled across endless space, no time to aimlessly drift,

Allow resolute dreams to dissipate, dissolve and die

Whip up wild passion, wonder of white swan

Newly taken flight; whirring of angel's wings.

Cosmic dancer, points, dazzling and bright,

With pinpoint precision, zeros in on true light.

Consumed by destiny, in charge of her fate,

Challenged, with elegance, to effortlessly elate.

UNLEASHED

Here stands a woman, strong, proud and brave,

Statuesque in beauty, gentle with grace;

Owns the attention, from others once craved.

Caring concern etched on her face

For all humanity's lost hopes and dreams;

Swept away on the winds of a long-forgotten time,

Buried in a morass of degradation, renegade schemes,

Her true essence recovered through ballerina rhyme.

Unleash the secret of who you really are,

Who stole your sparkle, left but a scar?

Leave them behind you, cut negative ties,

No space in this life for treachery and lies.

Joyfully reclaim your soft, creative soul,

Own your perfection; authentic, whole.

THE ART OF DOING NOTHING

There's really no need to strive and fear,

Let it all go, just sit here.

All by yourself, not pressurised, just alone,

To avoid interruption, turn off that phone!

You can just be, quietly sit,

Breathing healing energy in, allowing it,

Without the need for worry, stress or strain,

All that isn't giving you any gain.

This way, you are allowing peace

And inner calm to take the helm,

The ship is silent, your surroundings, balm.

Undulating peacefully on the waves,

Rising and falling, anchored in the deep enclaves.

Yet, ready to set sail, glide serenely over the water,

Isn't that the reason why you bought her?

There's no need to use brute force, once cast adrift,

Effortlessly, she holds her course. Buoyed up on the balmy

Sea, sails billowing, streamlined, surging cleanly forth.

Doesn't matter whether she's headed south or north.

Just know that when you are ready,

You will float forward, silently; steady.

Gently and easily, meld into your flow.

So, relax here, quietly. Drink in this scene.

One so calm, peaceful and serene.

Till once again ready to glide smoothly

Into life's slipstream.

WHO AM I?

I am the space that breathes life into your words,

I am the song, gloriously chirruped by birds,

I am the trees that stand tall and so proud,

I am the me that I trumpet out loud.

I am the music that lifts up the tune,

I am the light of the sun and the moon.

LOVE

Do great work; sow and nurture the seeds of positivity, purposefulness and joy...

URBAN KISS

Dark and edgy,

Teetering on the brink of urban sprawl.

The rocky road to our first kiss

Explodes into vibrant colour,

Now, tightly held; in thrall.

Silhouetted against the skyline,

Backs no longer pressed against the wall,

Merging deep into blissful eternity

As rainbow colours sublimely radiate,

And majestically fall.

THE WONDER OF LOVE

Love, in all its wondrous forms,

Radiates out, defies all norms.

True essence of beauty,

Sometimes involving loyalty, sense of duty.

Freely available to all, prepared, open to its call.

With gentle flowing cadence, washes away wounds,

Self-defence. Balmy, reassuring, sense of care,

Strengthens; magnifies all who dare

To open up their hearts.

THE WOMB

A world of hidden wonder

Resides resplendent in my womb,

A cocoon of nurture, security, protection,

No man could ever subsume.

There lies my burgeoning baby,

Suspended, warm and safe,

Oblivious to outer reality;

Daily churn and chafe.

Yet, imperceptibly,

Subterranean tremors permeate

Sacred space. Ripples of anxiety,

Apprehension, by osmosis,

Absorbs a trace.

Integrally connected,

By invisible umbilical cord,

Slumbering senses feel rejected,

When mother feels ignored.

Break free from protection,

Awaken from cushioned shell.

With overzealous enthusiasm,

Burst forth, release a piercing yell!

MY BEAUTIFUL, BONNY BABY

She's my beautiful, bonny baby,

And I just can't describe,

The boundless sense of joy I feel,

When I look deep into her eyes.

With love, I daily watch her,

As she does grow and stretch,

Swollen sense of motherly pride,

Sentimental tear, to my eye, does fetch.

The simplest things in life,

Lately hold a strange allure,

Hard fought ambition,

Flea-bitten; flies freely through the door!

Deep inside, I gaze;

To my sweet surprise, I find,

Being absent from my daughter,

Yes, I genuinely do mind!

Through her, spirit does teach me,

All I need to know and say,

She is my gleeful, gurgling, giggling girl;

Gorgeous in every way.

❖

LOVE

Love makes your heart sing,

Fly, on splendorous angel's wing,

Soar above base desire,

True love sets your soul on fire.

Flicker, ignite, fan the flame

Burning, passionately, in its name.

ALWAYS THERE

As I continue on my journey

You are always there,

Constant, patient, loyal

Alert and aware.

My companion, my friend,

Boundless bundle of joy,

Not afraid, at times,

A mournful stare to employ.

My supportive, silent shadow

Steadfast your gaze,

Paw prints on my heart,

Time will never erase.

LETTING GO

Surely, you will experience some discomfort as you stretch, far better than staying a self-defeating, self-pitying little wretch...

LABELS

Who am I?

What's in a name?

A wealth of criticism,

Hurt and shame.

It is a label,

Not who I am,

Yet, seek to erase it,

Feels a real sham.

Identifying with all you say,

Your taunts, your barbs,

Colouring not just my day,

But my life; emotion suppressed,

Stuffed down with carbs.

Negative thoughts,

Conquer, run rife,

Gently, this optimistic soul,

Absorbs unwelcome strife.

Unbidden, my confidence

Gallops west,

Yet my hurt stays silent,

Reigned in, clasped

Tight to my chest.

Inwardly subside,

Resist flow of tears,

Self-criticism canters,

Takes flight o'er the years.

Inadequate, insecure,

Unsure how to respond,

Walls closing in,

Lost in a slough of despond.

DIG DEEP

Dig defiantly into murky, forgotten depths.

Debased, disturbed;

Downtrodden, debilitated,

Yet, daring to be rehabilitated?

What devilish demon lurks here?

Languishing in dark, dank cave of doubt.

Blocked; claggy with sense of dread and fear,

Tightly sealed, light locked out.

Resistant to attempts at scrutiny;

Draw any nearer, and all my senses mutiny.

Breaking into a sweat, my pulse races.

Yet strangely oblivious to forgotten traces

Of sadness and woe; encountered aeons ago.

Sucked dry of ebb and flow.

Unforgiving; like rigid rock or belligerent boulder.

Magnified; a mountain to climb; Ben Nevis,

Without crampons, pickaxe and hook.

Craving clarity from any small crack or crevice.

My head strains to be shook,

Blown into a million different pieces

Shattered, shards scattered,

Explode that which solidity polices.

Desperate, a child; my sensitive mind

Sought self-defence.

Erupt; escape in explosion of effluence.

Heal, reveal; no more conceal

Femininity and flow.

Let go, release, no need to know each piece.

Accept the wonderful woman in you.

RELEASE, RELEASE

Release, release, I let you go,

Old hurts and desperation.

With my rapier, I cut a swathe,

Claim new hope and inspiration!

THE MASK REMOVED

Hello, world; it's me!

Unmasked. To remove

It, quite an ask.

Sensitive artist; healing, gentle,

Led me in movement,

Swaying, almost sentimental.

Washed away primeval fears,

Literally held too many years,

Side of me that seemed quite mental!

Painting done; mask still won.

That veil, stark outer cover,

Much of it, defence against my mother;

Other critics long ago; shadowy, forgotten foe.

Stubbornly, still block my flow.

Once again, gently clasping hands,

Led me to remove grasping bands,

Symbolically, shield peeled away,

No longer serves who I am today!

Heartfelt thanks, artist. Three cheers!

Hip, hip, hooray!

MOVEMENT

How to balance moving forward with consciously letting go,

At times, despite determination, progress seems so slow.

Lessons arise to teach me the value of soldiering on,

The ingenuity needed, once all ammunition is gone.

Which elements of life are truly done; shot through?

Regroup, review, plan; flexibly find new things to do.

Gather up knowledge, gained along the way,

Discern, discharge dusty debris, do it now, today!

I feel myself grow in stature, I have an army at my back,

Dedicated to the cause, whenever, I confess, I lack.

Strategise; focus on the future, on the bigger goal,

Ocean of blue and red, proudly uplift my soul!

Swell the ranks of camaraderie, companionship, compassion,

Share around the goodness, seemingly on ration.

I salute this fiery band, my loyal and trusty team,

Marching me out of the doldrums, to reclaim my dream.

FATHER'S DAY

Dad, you popped up unexpectedly on Father's Day,

Seemingly not there; locked away.

A faded memory, no longer seen,

Of a person, quiet, sensitive, calm; on the surface, so serene.

With an occasional, boyish, sense of humour,

Overlooking you, my own, neglectful, careless bloomer.

Unexpectedly, I espied a memorial rhyme,

On Facebook page, at exactly the right time,

To remember,

One who's birthday, 11 November,

Saw peace finally sealed on Armistice day.

Like the widely commemorated soldier, unknown,

Not one to shout out, complain or moan,

A generosity of gentle anonymity routinely held sway.

Unconcerned with antagonistic rumour, life's ups and downs

Zoning out when others yelled, or wore hostile frowns.

Yet in the background, always there,

Amenable, if you had a care.

Not always truly understanding,

Yet, ever calm, loyal and undemanding.

When the time came,

Slipped suddenly away from life's passing scene,

By your own downward demise; bewildered; seemed so mean.

A word that could never have been used to describe you.

AN AIRLOCK IN TIME

What is truth, what are lies?

All around insecurity flies.

Past life faces buried in me,

Stubborn, persistent, will not flee.

Strong, and silent, archetypal man,

Often feels like I am in his clan.

Loyalty, valour, doublet and hose,

Where lies history, when does it close?

I smell the taint of lost, spilled blood,

I feel treachery; betrayed, misunderstood.

Desperation seeps through me,

Where lies the fun? Where is my glee?

Banished when treason caused me to flee.

Flee from my home, flee from the land,

Flee from my people after one brave,

Persistent last stand.

I stand in my loyalty, I stood in my power,

Thwarted by betrayal, each day, every hour.

There's a time to let go, and a time to stand tall,

Yet how do I determine, whilst gripped tight in thrall?

Inside, a daunting dragon, vast mountain to climb,

Buried beneath this airlock in time...

SLAY THE LINEAGE

Dragons fight with all my might,

Clad in armour, daring knight.

Many men I've put to flight, still

Linger; shrouded in darkest night.

Insidiously clinging on; heartless, mean,

Clouding erstwhile sweetest dreams,

Clogging current hopes and schemes,

With long-forgotten derring-do.

Slay the lineage, clear the line.

Flagging, dragging past with me,

Battles, hangings, misery;

Slavery bred within family tree.

Slay the lineage, clear the line,

Whether a dandy, fearful fop,

When will it ever truly stop?

No more, pale, pathetic, milk-sop.

Slay the lineage, it's my time,

Cut across festering, sinister crime.

Slash through ancestors baying for blood,

Bless the ones that did most good.

Release the hate, let go of woe,

Firmly state "It's time to go".

Slay the lineage, clear the line.

Release the past, follow new signs.

Time to flourish, define my time,

My own desires and dreams.

No more bursting at the seams,

Knitting together muddled themes,

Filling pages, reams and reams,

With jaded hopes, wasted schemes.

Start a new chapter, milky white,

Slay the lineage, rewrite my life!

ENDINGS

I miss you.

Deep in my heart;

Our friendship. Sharing

Warmth and love;

Affection. Now facing

Rejection. Feeling

Futile.

We came together,

A meeting of minds;

End of facing harsher

Times. Wading through

Treacle. Intimate moments,

Shared hurts, exploration.

A journey to replenish the soul.

Seeking succour, beauty sprang

From tentative beginnings.

Laughter, fun, creative expression.

Learning lessons, side by side.

Now, no longer abide

Cloying closeness.

Caged birds, hemmed in,

Desire release.

Set free, independently

Soar across boundless skies

Of infinite possibility.

WEIGHED DOWN

Why don't I clear my closet?

Let go of coat and hat;

Bag up saggy trousers,

Other appalling old tat!

A congestion of clothes;

Ranging from small to extra-large.

In danger of choosing the wrong ones,

Spoiling my décolletage!

Why don't I clear my closet?

Once sylphlike, wore many a transparent gown,

Long since I've expanded,

Prefer to stay under my eiderdown!

Will I ever diet,

Return to being slim?

Strangely, all that's missing,

Are clothes to wear to the gym!

Why don't I clear my closet?

Declutter, make ample space?

The minute I stop simply dreaming,

My future wishes will gather pace!

SHINE FOR ME

As you remember me this day,

Let sweetness blend with sorrow,

You are my gift,

Left on this earth,

To create a brighter tomorrow.

And, as you ever blossom and grow,

My legacy lives on;

So be my light,

Within this world,

Through you, still brightly shone.

THE TUDOR GALLERY

Piercing, soulful, benevolent; cold,

Those eyes, my attention hypnotically hold.

Boldly gazing across the ages,

Fascinating array of kings, queens, seers and sages.

Masterful, aloof, virile; sallow-complexioned, careworn, kind,

Paint bedecked canvas compellingly captures those left
behind.

I see life, essence captured, distilled.

Living, almost breathing presence, timeless, fulfilled.

Soul connection, given hue, in a gallery, centuries later, I stare
at you

With awe and wonder, a strength of feeling, deep and true.

Magnetically, I connect with those

Proudly shod in doublet and hose,

Or bedecked in luxuriantly sewn, beaded, bejewelled dresses,

Headpieces adorning sculpted tresses.

Here and there a frown; careworn brow,

Energetically transported, so real, then as now.

Mesmerised by how, within that multi-coloured hue,

Artists truly captured soul of you.

I gaze upon a man, appears so kind.

Lo! On hand-engraved plaque, I find,

Written description bears out artist's depiction,

A peacemaker, dedicated, intentions sincerely fine,

The Enneagram, would surely reveal a number nine?

I salute you, Tudor statesman, your number is the same as mine!

THE DIVINE TAPESTRY OF LIFE

We are integral strands of this divine tapestry; "Life".

Golden threads of humanity; intricately interwoven,

Entwining hope, vibrant joy, with the dull, distant ache

Of despair; heavy heartache of letting go.

A tapestry, tinged with subtle streaks of sadness,

Stitched through with yearning; illusion of something more.

Magical beyond the realms of pure imagination,

Yet hanging calmly, peaceful, timeless, upon the wall.

EMERGENCE

As you experience movement, create life-changing shifts, you will, newly emboldened, dare to share your gifts...

NOTHING TO SAY

Nothing to say,

Nowhere to be,

Just sitting here,

Quietly, being me.

No need to worry,

No need to fear,

I trust that all I need

Resides in here.

I am a being

A creature of light,

I lay down my weapons

No longer to fight.

I am a woman,

I was a child,

Not an evil monster

Forever reviled.

Hurts from millennia

Buried away,

Leaving me speechless

Yet with so much to say.

I am reality, I am truth

No longer scarred by naivety of youth.

SPRING FREE

Spring free.

Release unbidden

Burdens that hold

Me captive;

Shadows of a darker

Past.

Spring free.

Joyously gambol

In the rich lushness;

A verdant new

Beginning.

MELT POLAR ICE CAPS

Melt, polar ice caps of your mind.

Allow them to break, crumble, flow,

Gathering momentum,

Tumultuous thoughts

Gush; rush forward,

Blast through limitations.

Sweeping through the mire,

Wash away rigidity.

Splashes of desire

Inspire movement, pace.

Empowering energy, strength,

Race forward.

Released, abandoned;

Spinning ice floe,

Swirling, washed around

Thunderous rolling river,

Foaming, rushing, pushing,

Erupts, spews forth

Bubbling purpose.

Yet, damned despair,

Impetus crashes,

Jolting, halting,

Converging, merging.

Icey cold, concealed,

No ice pick revealed.

Slabs of doubt solidify.

Who am I

To be powerful, strong?

Released from this straitjacket.

Gentle nurture, sweet caress,

Playful ripple, forward flow,

Eradicates crash and blow,

Allows a trickle, sparkle,

Inner essence, elixir;

Naturally to grow.

A BLANK PAGE

Faced with a blank page; my future, my life.

Staring back at me, taunting me; I stall at the enormity

Of this clarion call for creation. Hesitant mark appeared,

Blemishes pristine whiteness? Or a blessing? Venture

Forth, unleash meaning and mission, magnificence and joy.

The embodiment of all that I am, all that I can be,

Committed to paper, for all to see.

Or cowardly, baulk at this honour?

The ultimate power to create a flamboyant future,

Shine beacon-like; showcase my very essence.

Sweep through swathes of darkness,

With irrevocable light.

Beauty of life; teaming possibility.

Swimming with the tide; in flow.

Thoughts, words and deeds undulate.

Soul expression in motion,

Surges tumultuously into life.

WORDS MATTER

Words anger, words heal,

Words true inner essence reveal.

Words of wisdom, truth and grace,

Timeless beauty, etched on your face.

A shrug, a sigh, a careworn frown;

Expressionless, world-weary, worn down.

When negative words are flying around,

You lose the Empress, wear the crown

Of thorns, pain and sorrow; endless

Crying over lost tomorrows.

Choose wisely; my plea to you.

Uplifting words, bathed in glorious hue,

Splashed imaginatively, like artist's paint.

Glorious inner portrait, not sad reflection; full of taint.

Sever ties with endless ache; imagine

Ingredients of a perfect cake, hidden depths,

Crystal clarity of tranquil lake. Bathe in a mountain

Stream, float carefree in a dream,

Clouds billowing, gentle, free.

Ask yourself, implicitly,

Which words best describe me?

FLOWING FREE

One drop starts the flow.

Plops gently onto the paper.

Rolls around, jelly-like, tentatively

Testing the boundaries, this brave

New world of whiteness.

A splash of enthusiasm follows

Hot on its heels, triumphantly

Lands, skids, merges and expands.

Amoeba-like, stretches and grows.

Delighted drips drop by,

Pitter, patter, joyously chatter,

What does it matter if they cause

A splatter, uniformity they defy.

A gregarious gush, gathers force,

Free flowing, dancing and growing,

Tumbles and tussles, flexes its muscles,

Crashes cavalierly on its course.

LOCKED AWAY

Buried deep, locked away,

Secrets, silence;

So much to say.

You are a beacon,

A being of light,

Yet you've lost your voice

Given up on the fight.

You are a miracle about to be reborn,

You are the shoe, not the shoehorn;

Fighting to make everything fit

When there's no end, no container for it.

Release true essence, unleash potent power,

Joyously all around, gentle raindrops shower.

Cascading down, caress soft, fertile ground,

With a wondrous, ethereal sound;

The clarion call of the newly crowned.

THE GRAND CANYON

I teeter on the brink.

The majestic chasm

Gapes gloriously

Around me;

Breath-taking, expansive;

Its rock-bound brilliance

Stillness personified.

Aeons of spiritual wisdom

Etched in sentient strands

Densely crown

Stalwart outcrops

of Colorado-carved canyon.

Gazing anew at pure grandeur,

Poised; staring into the abyss,

Strains of glorious greatness

Stir stubbornly within my chest.

Engulfed with the wisdom of the elders

I contemplate pure bliss.

Eager as the eagle,

My soul and senses soar,

Launched into the vastness,

No longer at safety claw.

Recklessness reverberates

As I release a MIGHTY ROAR!

AWAKENING

Life is truly meant for us to live; by our own
expression, give to those, like us, who have
sometimes been squashed, ignored, or diligently
working; self-effacing, behind a screen of
uniformity...

AWAKEN

Woman, oh woman, know what you did;

Your light under a bushel, of duty, you hid.

Break free from constraint, cast off those chains,

Shake off the shackles, re-engage your brain.

Women, rise again, filled with fresh hope.

Untie the knot, gently, uncoil the rope.

No longer constrict that elegant throat.

Undo those handcuffs, that make the blood boil,

Rise up from the ashes of oppression and toil.

Dance, Aphrodite, in streams of golden sunlight!

Not designed to whimper, quiver and cower.

Glory in your purpose, brilliant and bright,

Grounded, centred; claim inner power.

Devour the fire, strength reignite.

Unleash the Empress, true Goddess within,

Reject misplaced shame, guilt of original sin.

Bite into juicy apple, sit content in the bower,

A bud, a teardrop, dew on a flower,

Removed from oppression of judgemental glower.

Bloom, glorious Goddess of wisdom, truth and love,

Shower true essence, bathed in white light from above.

Relish the challenge, intent to be, have and do,

Rise one and all, claim true beauty in you.

RIDING THE CAROUSEL

Round in circles, round I go;

Sometimes fast, sometimes slow.

How on earth will I ever know

That I've reached my destination?

Along the way, I experience signs,

Tiny touches, so divine.

A moment shared, a word, a lesson

An uplifting quote, someone's blessing.

Someone stops me to review,

Whispers "I believe in me, I believe in you."

I take a breather, drink in the view

Perhaps you relate, have been there too?

Yet, once again, mount the carousel,

My trusty steed knows this route so well.

And whilst we gallop gently to the music,

My sense of purpose, somehow, I lose it.

Ideas, ideas, swirl around,

Will I ever dismount this merry-go-round?

Multifaceted, magnificent, creatively inspired,

Yet not grounded, feeling "wired".

Now you've seen me, stilled the wheel,

Taken your place alongside on your saddle.

No more allow my genius to be concealed,

Thrown a lifeline; allowed to paddle.

CREATING SPACE

Clear out that clutter,

Get rid, get rid, get rid!

All of the old junk that you have hid

In cupboards; underneath the bed,

Brazenly building up, blocking your head!

Pull out those drawers,

Shake out those sheets,

Gather that jumble,

Hidden beneath your seats.

Seek out what you squirrelled away in a bid,

To hide your extravagance; cost at least fifty quid!

Now it's discovered, forlorn and unused,

How you came to forget it, you just feel confused.

Clear out that clutter, don't resist and mutter.

For once you free up significant space,

Your mood will brighten; with joy, you will utter

As renewed creativity, you effortlessly embrace.

ROOM TO WRITE

Your office, newly sorted,

Re-enter the fray.

Tackle unruly contents

Of neglected in-tray!

Let imagination wander,

As you pause to sit and stare,

Perhaps a lurid story

Will open up its lair?

Fiery the dragon,

Flaunting orange breath.

Perhaps a gallant knight,

Saves damsel from certain death?

Or a dreamy lover,

Muscle-bound, leather-clad,

Seduces elegant lady;

Will he be unveiled a cad?

However, you choose to write it,

It will come to pass,

So, lift your spirits high,

And get writing, lass!

OPPORTUNITIES

Opportunities, opportunities, softly tapping at my door,

A smattering of hope, yet, wait; I've been here before.

Consistently coaxing, "Let me in", "Let me in",

Why does being bold, grasping life, seem such a sin?

A surge of apprehension, an undertow of fear,

Why do they beckon to me? Why don't I want to hear?

Dive in, swim through the rapids, confident and clear,

What is it that stops me? How do I draw them near?

Opportunities, opportunities, knocking persistently at my door,

Begin to invade my senses, "Listen to me", ardently implore.

Pronounce, "Open up", "Open up", you know that we are here,

Be brave, be bold; listen, we urge you, respond and hear.

Opportunities, opportunities, rapping rapaciously at my door,

No more escape, we command you; venture out, explore!

Tear back that bolt, release, deftly turn the key.

Announce to the world, "I am here, the true, authentic me".

Free in all my glory, I proudly claim the hour,

I grasp my opportunities, I'm standing in my power!

❖

COIN

Life turns on a coin,
Spin causes shift
Turned on its head,
Creating uplift!

❖

BEAUTIFUL BEAMS OF HUMANITY

You are a shining stream of sunlight,

A brilliant, beautiful sight,

Shimmering, shifting, dancing,

Sparkling with pure delight.

Bountifully, vital, vibrant essence of you,

Bursts through the gathering gloom,

Darting, dazzling energy lifts saggy spirits;

Slumped, resigned within the room.

You engulf each person present with a glorious golden glow,

Warmth and love emerge, until now buried deep below.

Boundless, abundant brilliance of heart-warming humanity,

Envelops all with sunny strength, renewing their sanity.

CREATIVE SELF-EXPRESSION

You are a beacon, burning bright, birthed to emerge, grow, and shine your inner light...

BANISH YOUR BLUES!

Grab a handy paintbrush,

Allow it to run rife!

Paint a vivid picture,

Penetrate your life.

A riot of rampant colour,

Redolent, raw and real,

Infiltrate inhibitions,

Reality reveal.

Wash away woeful worries,

Banish boring brown,

Obliterate with wild flurries,

Remnants of careworn frown.

Decorate possessions,

Daub as if possessed,

Splatter vivid colour,

Plaster over past regrets.

Relish rainbow revelations,

Brush away those blues!

Claim your inner artist,

Garnish with glowing, garish hues!

WORDS, WORDS, WORDS

Words, words, words.

Scrawled on bits of paper,

Corkscrewing through your hair,

Etched upon the table top,

Scrunched up on the stairs.

Slip-sliding down the bannister,

Dilly-dallying in the hall,

Words, words, words;

Playful, having a ball!

Words, words, words.

Read sleepily, in the morning,

With a cup of reviving builder's tea;

Enveloping your dinner;

Succulent fish and chips, with glee!

Drift off during daydreams,

Form frantic fantasies at night;

Words, words, words,

Pick up your pen; take flight!

Words, words, words,

Scald you when naughty,

Caress, when loving and carefree,

Connect across the spaces,

The silent you and me.

A graceful gavotte,

Dance, brazen in the breeze,

Always respond "Bless you"

To an unexpected sneeze!

Words, words, words,

Forever your brain will tease!

POETIC LICENCE

I carry a poetic licence, permitting me to expand

On reality, experience duality; venture boldly

Into new realms. Embellish, relish the challenges

Dreamed up through vivid imagination.

Not bound by convention; glean new meaning.

Invent, distort, contort into fantastical illusion,

Or being taut, cut through all delusions.

Tucked away, in innocuous plaid pocket,

Till once more brought out to play, sweeps me away,

With promise of golden, bejewelled locket.

A dance of dreams, of whirlwind schemes,

A gymnast gracefully glancing off the beams,

With a poetic licence reams and reams of possibility

Unfold; of heroes bold, beauty beyond measure,

Pirates sailing windswept seas, in search of buried treasure.

Where I espy beauty, it is my duty

To magnify tenfold. Not to lie, but do or die.

Pen is my brush, verdant, lush. Strokes

Of tumultuous passion, splurge and splash,

As nib does flash, without a care for fashion.

Jauntily, I play, till dark dragons slay

With creative self-expression.

FACEBOOK FANTASIES

Dawn breaks; gradually awake.

Sit and stretch, contemplate.

Thoughts and feelings seeping through

Careless memories, echoes of you.

Idly, on Facebook, take a look.

What friend's comments strike a chord,

What inspiration to be took?

Aimlessly browsing, casually see

New "friendly" face, unknown to me.

On her page, a rousing poem,

For essence of new year, inspiration

Growing. A confident companion

In raw self-expression, her light

Burns brightly, no dull compression.

Passion, wise words, expressed on a page,

Communication for an insightful

Dawning new age. Release anger, negative

Thoughts, assuage ennui, Facebook posts

Unlock quick curiosity in me.

Connection, creativity begin to flow;

Go to linked artist, her animal art page.

Location, inspiration, ideas cascade;

Tumble forth, somersault one after another.

Harlequin nimbly parades, sleek

In jumpsuit, mystery mask,

Proclaims, "It's all here, you up to the task?"

Wonderful, in bed, to sit and bask,

Yet, as momentum gathers fast,

Rolling rapidly o'er mud and grass,

I cry, "Stop awhile, alas,

How will my poor brain bring such

Splendour to pass?"

Rollicking rumbles; tumbling,

Careering off piste, yet desire in me,

Passion for life, released!

Later cries out for practical plan,

For now, frantic squiggles

Signal endless élan!

A SWIRL OF CREATIVITY

Who says it can't be easy,

Constant struggle to be free,

Crushed grape of creativity,

Not full-bodied wine it's meant to be.

The vine, gnarled and knotted,

Grapes plucked, placed in a pot,

Ripened richness, squishing,

Squashing; trampled underfoot.

Inky, luscious liquid, soon fills the water butt.

Swishing and swirling, allowed space to breathe.

Unleash latent feelings, left underground to seethe.

Bottled up tight, beneath metal bottle-top,

Constricted energy creates a glottal stop.

Smooth flowing river of life,

Spinning in the glass,

Sloshing and swooshing,

Stirring up a morass

Of compressed, creative urges,

Captive in the throat,

Unleash hidden flavour,

Buried bouquet,

Each soft, delicate note.

Fortified with flavonoids,

Embodying ripeness and hope,

Vibrant blood-red energy cascades,

Slides smoothly, solicitously down the slopes.

Richness and flow, soothes the sorry sides,

Caresses rampant joy; deep in my heart resides.

Rich, red river, flowing within my veins,

Velvety sensuality, arises, gloriously unrestrained.

Tangy, fruity richness, matured upon the vine,

Longing for release, for freedom I now pine.

A yearning and an aching, arise within my chest,

A rich garland of glorious scent and colour.

My cup overflows with vibrancy, I know I can cope;

Unleash my inner brilliance, a beacon of light and hope.

Let inhibitions perish, creative expression release,

"In vino veritas", may it never cease!

GRATITUDE

I allow gratitude to flow freely

Like a fountain,

Forever ebbing and flowing;

The emotions engulf me,

I allow myself to feel,

To explore, to revel

In a never-ending stream

Of consciousness…

Turn on the tap,

Release, cascade;

Shimmering and gushing,

Translucent, foaming,

Falling over itself

With the joy of freedom,

Self-expression,

Water of life,

Adapting, growing.

Defenceless, I dive

Deliriously into the deep

Blue yonder.

Swirl and swim in an ocean

Of endless possibilities,

Allow the grace of gratitude

To wash over me,

Through me,

I am whole.

ENCAPSULATED IN THE CLOUDS

Sleep-induced visions, ousted by swirling streaks of genius,

Float majestically across impassive, bloodshot sky.

Effortlessly, expression soars, softly spans opulent ocean.

Eager eddies of excitement, embodied in a pulsating pure-bred stallion.

A mystical charioteer, clear-sighted, clasps the reigns. Blazing

a brazen trail of rhythmic newness, bursts forth into the fray.

Creativity careers forward in a whorl of wind, wit and wonder,

Vibrant, alive, electrified by the power of endless possibility.

Fiery flames fan the dawning drama of a new day;

Transform dreamy notions into radiant, radical, reality.

FEMININE POWER

As others bask in your new golden glow, it helps for them, also to know, that they have their own miracles to perform...

RECLAIMING ME

This is me, it's who I am; sick and tired

Of feeling a sham. I claim my courage, face

My fear, break through constriction of society;

Self-imposed limits, those initiated by you, mummy dear.

It's taken so long for me to find out, conquer

Interminable worry, dread and doubt.

Gain a sense of my genuine feelings,

Not bound by expectations, sending me reeling.

I've carried a heavy burden incredibly long,

A yearning to impress, fit in, belong.

Yet, how can I be truly accepted,

When my sense of self is not at all strong?

I've taken time out to search and explore,

Investigate habitual refrain of "poor, unloved

Little me". Playing the victim kept me safe,

Conditioned by restrained reality.

Now I recognise the power of my own thought,

Subconscious nature I was never taught. Express

Myself authentically, not how "I ought". Honesty,

Truth, legitimacy; sometimes struggle; often fly free.

One thing I know for sure, the more I continue

To embrace my feelings, create a life I adore,

Continuously claim the inner me, I truly experience

How magical living a multifaceted life can be!

THE OPEN ROAD

Today I take the wheel.

No longer wait for other clowns

To critique the ups and downs

Of my life.

I am the driver, I seize the wheel,

I pay for the gas, I seal the deal.

I embrace the freedom of the open road,

No longer back-seat driver allowed to goad.

I turn the switch, I select the station,

Which words or music suit my destination.

I choose the direction, I plan the route,

Playfully, I give my horn a toot!

Straight to the point, or meandering free,

Mine is the path that seizes opportunity.

At a crossroads, I read the signs,

I may decide not to travel in straight lines.

Occasionally, I stop, pick up a fellow traveller,

Chat, banter, share the load, help to unravel her

Golden dreams. Sisterhood often means

Greater success in our shared hopes and schemes.

Back at the wheel, I travel on alone,

With all the resources, I claim as my own.

My inner toolbox will carry me far,

I am the owner, I choose the car.

I am the driver, I take the wheel,

I travel in whichever direction I feel.

A FEMININE FANFARE

Surreptitiously, my senses surrender,

Suffused in a sensory symphony of soft power.

Caressed, cocooned in creative consciousness,

I yield to the splendid sweep of divine sacred energy.

A feminine fanfare of feelings radiates;

Dances in the exquisite afterglow.

WE GATHER

We gather, loud and proud. No longer bowed

Down by the weight of centuries.

We cry, we weep, emotions seep from careworn crevices,

Sweeping away worries and woes.

We know our time has come, we know we must beat

Our drum and dance till dawn.

Forlorn no more, reborn to adorn mother earth's grassy plateaus,

With open arms we joyously sway, embrace life.

YOUR SIGNATURE SUCCESS STORY

Join us, celebrate, before it gets too late!

Don't allow enthusiasm to abate,

Success is there for you to take,

Please don't leave it too near your wake,

Really something to contemplate…

What makes you truly unique?

The way you walk, or how you speak?

Wisdom and knowledge shared in a book,

The daring deeds, the risks you took?

Raising a boisterous family;

A high-powered career; high visibility?

Do you feel you've reached your peak?

Or more fulfilment dare to seek?

When do you experience playfulness, fun?

Are there tall tales still to be spun?

A new adventure, mountain to climb?

Perhaps you're thinking "It's **my** time"?

We all have our signature moves,

Our distinctive rhythm, beat and grooves,

We each define our own success,

Perhaps by reclaiming, renaming our "mess"!

What are **your** ingredients for Signature Success?

How best with the world your gifts express?

Now is the time to claim your feminine power,

And into the world, your true essence shower.

Capture your story, uncover your true voice,

How you employ it, that's your own choice.

Whether in family, community, a book, or on-screen,

Now is the time for you to shine, be seen!

WOW-FULL WOMEN, IGNITE YOUR LIGHT!

Two hundred women; closeted in creative conference room.

Oh, how their divine energy can lift the gathering gloom;

Experienced outside in rampant rain, rising flood.

Inside, spirituality at work, inspiring genuine good!

Surrender to an aura of positive, purposeful intent,

Swelled by chatter and laughter; the atmosphere rent

With the amazing energetic alchemy, of love and acceptance,

True feminine essence of you and me.

If, afterwards, it stirs up your "stuff",

Observe and learn, what makes you feel rough?

There's a yearning to release from deep inside,

No longer need for inner goddess to hide!

Doubts, regrets, dread and fear,

Let each one out, welcome them here.

They are ready to heal and go,

Allowing authentic inner spirit to shine and grow!

As we say farewell to this gathering bright,

Which turned up the volume of spiritual light,

Wow-full women, awakening to live their dreams!

Way forward for this world, it seems,

Dalai Lama got it right,

Will be Western women, shining bright!

I SEE YOU

I see you, women of the world.

I see your glory, feel your pain;

I sense your loss, celebrate your gains.

I feel your sadness, hidden joy,

I rejoice in the gifts you daily employ.

Join together; rise, sisters, rise,

Send fervent wishes soaring to the skies.

Realise your dreams, claim your power;

Appreciate every day, each emerging hour.

Empathy, care, freedom, fun;

Completing tasks that need to be done.

Thank the Lord for what you have:

Partners, friends, family, community,

With whom you connect, create true unity.

Rise as women, alongside men,

It's not a case of "us against them".

Hold the space, grasp the reigns,

Softly stroll down country lanes.

Own your inner, feminine gifts;

Create new meaning, life-changing shifts.

Stand up and speak your authentic truth,

Silenced so cruelly in your youth.

Easing into grace and flow,

Allow your energy to expand and grow.

Sensitive, gentle, courageous, strong,

Within you, gratitude, joy, belong.

Regain your true essence, inner worth,

This is what will save the earth.

Allow past hurts to fade and die,

Claim your inner reason "why".

Achieving balance, grounded, real,

Allow your own thoughts, desires to feel,

Nor your pain, your hurts conceal.

When with overwhelm, doubts you reel,

Look around, you're not alone,

For decades women have been coming home.

I see you, you are not alone,

I see you, as a woman, not a drone,

I see you, my Queen, reclaim your throne.

CELEBRATION

Too often we forget to celebrate.

We go about our tasks, move from one to the next,

Become irate, frazzled, suddenly vexed,

Perhaps it's because we left it too late to celebrate.

To achieve takes time. There is reason in the rhyme,

Rhyme in our reason. Constant as the changing season,

Life moves on. Little time to revisit, ponder on, how creative

Flow addresses, those intricacies, our successes.

Stand back, admire the view, as artist purveys

Oil-fuelled hue. Gaze anew, in awe and wonder,

At the brush strokes fine, reflected shine of golden gown.

I dare you, smile, appreciate, disown that jaundiced frown.

Celebrate with pride. Before you resurrect your easel,

Pick up your fork, garnish your glass; "pop" goes the weasel!

Dance, rejoice, shout and sing, invite your friends to join right in.

It's in the celebration of our gifts that the wisest truly win!

CELEBRATING YOU

Celebrating you, who you really are,

Every little blemish, hurt, cut and scar.

Women, you have travelled, so very, very, far,

Learned there's no need to discard and burn your bra!

You have within you, everything you need;

Tenacity and talent, ability to breed.

Nurture, and love, everyone you feed;

Not forgetting yourself, receive, do not concede.

Celebrate your mothers, remember who you are,

Often, they could not drive their own car.

Travesties, injustice, resentment buried deep,

Gather all together, throw them in a heap.

Burn them on the brazier, chuck them on the fire,

You are a woman, stand in your power.

Watch old hurts smoulder, flames leap higher and higher.

You alone can claim your yearning heart's desire.

You are not an effigy, a plastic Barbie doll,

Don't deserve to be blackened by a troll,

Playing cards; you always come up trumps.

Don't let lewd comments drag you down into the dumps.

Talent, caring, creativity; yes, you also have a bust,

But not intended solely, as the subject of lust.

You can choose the outcome, you can sow the seed,

Yours is the decision, whether or not to conceive.

You can do the shopping, you can push the pram,

But only when you say; "This is not solely who I am".

I am a human being, whole in my own right,

I claim the facility for some well-deserved respite".

I fight my own battles, good as any man,

My choice of weapons, not just pots and pans.

I use wit and wisdom, anger when its due,

I stand up, I count, just as much as you.

I can be a tomboy, or a "girlie girl",

I decide whether or not my hair will curl,

If colours, make-up, lipstick, I duly choose,

I can decide whether or not they match my shoes!

I am an intellectual, I am unique,

I have a voice, I stand up and speak.

I am understanding, I am not a sham,

I am a lady, yet, sometimes a "Madame".

Ladies, we are rising; no longer considered a crime,

It is not surprising, finally, it's our time!

ABOUT THE AUTHOR

Aged 51, Sue Williams took early retirement from her career with the Civil Service, having worked in career information, advice and guidance services for adults for over 21 years. Her own early career aspirations were thwarted when she felt too lacking in confidence to explore a career in journalism during her late teens. Unsure of what else to do, she initially took a teacher training course, and later retrained, achieving her Diploma in Careers Guidance in 1991.

On leaving employment, Sue embarked on a journey of exploration, during which she began to write morning pages (a technique for unlocking creative self-expression), which led to her writing in rhyme! She has since published, and is lead author in, two anthologies of true stories aimed at inspiring women to have more self-belief and confidence; *Believe You Can* and *Believe You Can Succeed*. She has created a set of inspirational Believe cards, which are also available as an award-winning app on Google Play and iTunes.

Sue ran her first major event for women, "*Your Signature Success Story*", in 2016.

 For more information, please go to Sue's website:

www.sue-williams.com.

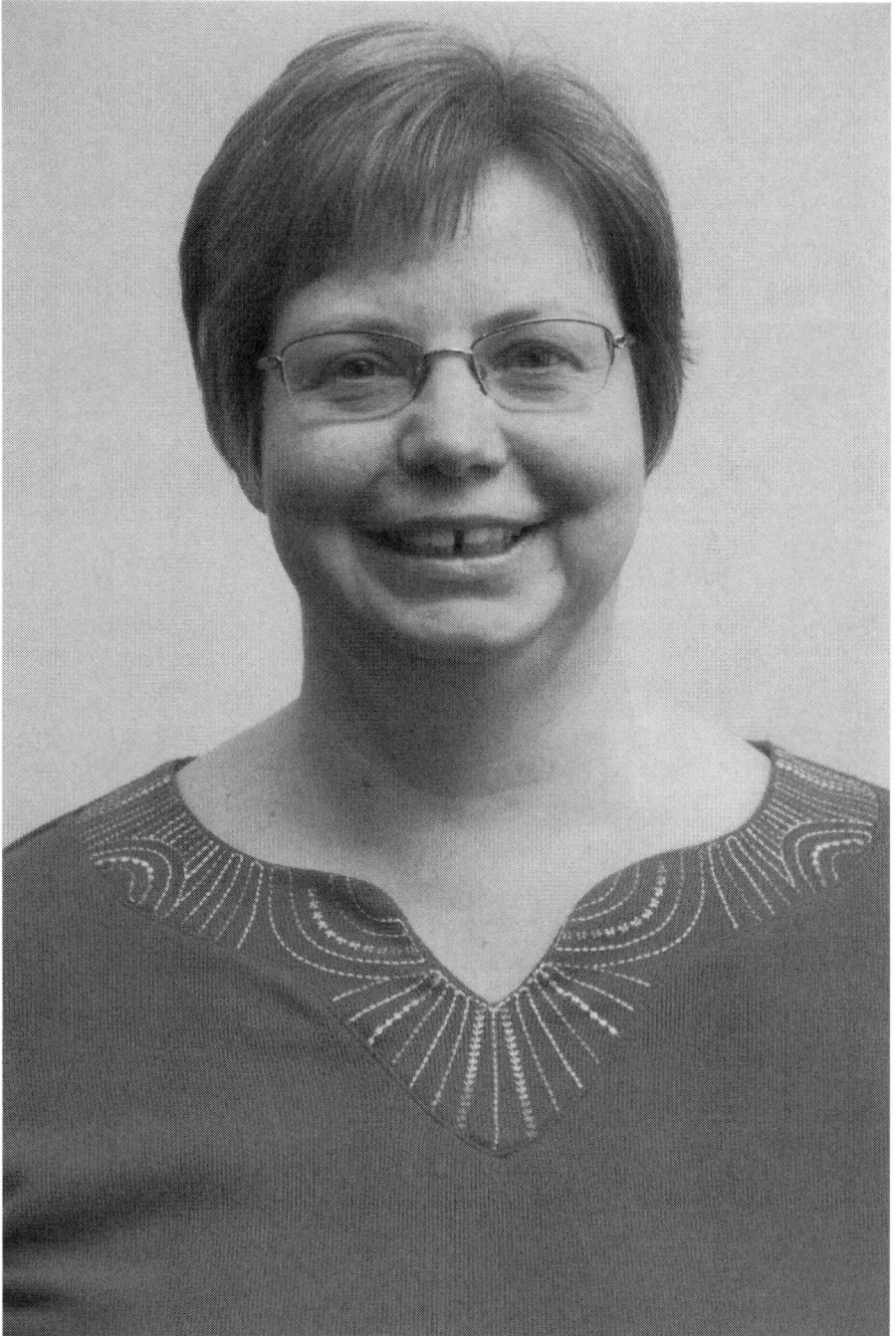

ABOUT THE FRONT COVER – THE MASK

As I listened to the announcement of the death of David Bowie, I looked up in shock from my book. Instantly, I found myself gazing at a portrait of my own colourful, daubed face looking intently back at me from my bedroom wall. In that moment, it was as if in a mystical whoosh, time expanded and contracted, and a sudden realisation hit me... he and I had started at opposite ends of some invisible scale, yet in this split second, we felt connected through a bizarre "touch point" in time.

What do I mean by this? As a shy, sensitive teenager, growing up in the 1970s, I had found much of what David Bowie was experimenting with to be quite disturbing. The idea of Aladdin Sane and the howling of Diamond Dogs unsettled me. Bowie's chameleon-like changes of appearance left me baffled, and a little unnerved.

Yet, fast forward to my fifties and here I was staring at a picture of my face, daubed with vibrant blues, oranges, pinks and greens! Symbolic, perhaps, that it is never too late to experiment, and to come out from under the masks we wear. Or, at least, to try on newer, more expressive ones, and uncover different facets of ourselves! This creative, playful approach, whether physically applying paint to ourselves, trying out new movements or dance, changing our clothes, or simply playing with colour and words on a page, helps to release the hidden feelings we often keep locked deep within.

The picture on the front cover was the result of my participation in a clown face painting session. Two of the poems describing that session are contained in this book. I chose this picture of the mask as the cover for a number of reasons. It feels like a landmark in my own unique journey to self-expression. It is a bold image, and one that does not appeal to everyone. I have received reactions about it ranging from "it is too scary", "too masculine", "too messy" to praise for how it stands out, and makes a bold statement. For me, it seems to encapsulate a sense of many of the poems in this collection.

I have come to realise how the encumbrance of expectations has coloured my family history, particularly the handicap my mother felt at not having been born a boy. The mask is a pastiche of the jumble of experiences good and bad that constitute life. Above all, a sense of vibrant hope shines through. When the artist Juliette Jeanclaude asked my opinion of the image, my initial response was ambivalent. She took a step backwards, paused, reflected, then joyously remarked on the sailboats she could see gliding gaily across the blue of my eyes!

Sue Williams

SUE WILLIAMS' BOOKS - AVAILABLE ON AMAZON

BELIEVE YOU CAN SUCCEED – 21 True Stories to Inspire Entrepreneurs

BELIEVE YOU CAN – Face Your Fears and Confidently Claim the Life You Desire

BELIEVE ORACLE CARDS

Available on Google Play and Apple App Store

Believe

You Can Succeed!

21 True Stories
to Inspire
Entrepreneurs

Edited by

Sue
Williams

Believe You Can!

Face Your Fears and Confidently Claim the Life You Desire

Edited by

Sue Williams

25155156R00081

Printed in Great Britain
by Amazon